LABYRINTH

N. CHINIR

First published in 2020 by
BecomeShakespeare.com

One Point Six Technologies Pvt Ltd,
123, Building J2, Shram Seva Premises,
Wadala Truck Terminus,
Wadala (E), Mumbai - 400037
T:+91 8080226699

ISBN: 978-93-5438-022-8

ACKNOWLEDGEMENTS

To God, for his amazing grace and unfailing love;

To my parents, who I owe everything to, I am thankful for the immense support they have given.

To Chingneihlam Zou for being there for me, through thick and thin and having faith in me when I doubted myself, I am deeply grateful to you.

Not forgetting the strangers who I came across in the streets and cafes; I have written poems about the stories your eyes held, may you find yourself within these pages.

Credits:

I would take this opportunity to thank Prerana Saikia for the beautiful cover art, her IG handle is: @blue.heeah, also to Diarchy Hajong, @ darchyhajong for his illustrations.

PREFACE

Poetry is the language of the soul; these collections of poems are a depiction of human emotions.

It's of ambition, love, romance, passion, Darkness, loss, self-love, dreams, self-realization and above all, of faith.

Growing up in this era isn't easy, I thank my stars that let me stumble upon old poems; they have helped my soul regain its ground and taught me a thing or two about life.

Some poems will reflect dreams that are as ambitious as the glaring Sun; some will depict the darkness we all struggle to keep at bay; may you find yourself in this Labyrinth.

My hope and wish is that someone out there somewhere stumbles upon these poems of mine and it gives them strength and courage and assurance that they are not alone in this labyrinth we call life.

An aspiring poet, a young graduate who is trying his best to achieve his dreams, in a world filled with chaos.

Realist

You say you don't believe in magic!

Yet everyday you'd cast spells upon yourself

Convincing yourself that you aren't good enough

But what if I tell you a secret;

A revelation that everything you see around you,

Was once made of nothing but thoughts.

N. Chinir

Nothing is more beautiful than two broken people;

Loving each other with everything they have…

N.Chinir

She stopped taking leaps of "faith".

Her heart was like her wings.

She once flew too close to the sun.

Although her feathers grew back and her heart "healed".

And although her wings were so beautiful,

She was scared to fly again!

She had a beautiful heart

That was scared of falling in love…

N. Chinir

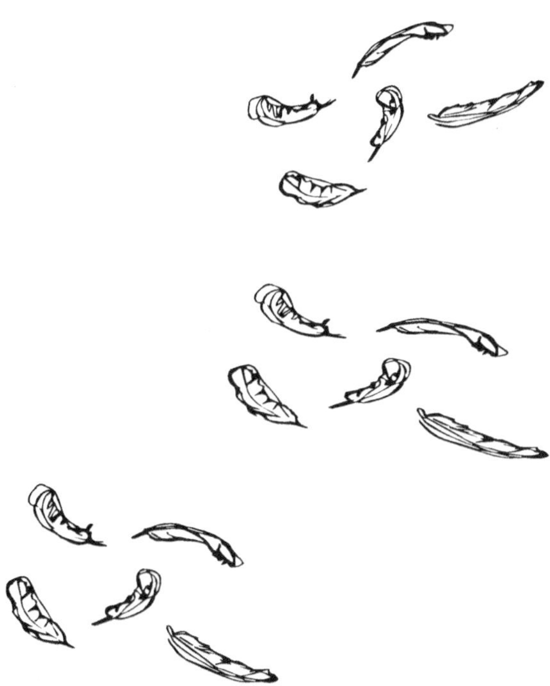

She advised "If you ever have to mourn for a living person,

You just need to dig six feet deep

And write all the words and promises they once said

And bury them and maybe leave a white rose for dramatic effects,

You know so that the dead stay dead,

That's how we move on when we don't want them dead" she laughed...

N Chinir

You yearn for a love so strong that it could match the storms,

So deep that it would eclipse the oceans,

A love that puts a smile every morning

But even if I promised you the heavens,

You couldn't dare take a step forward;

Let alone bring down your walls…

N Chinir

'*Obsession*'

Our crime was, we had dreamt

Dreams so wild, so fierce and ambitious,

That the gods saw it as arrogance,

But little did they know that it was already too late…

We had already fallen madly in love with the Sun,

We had already vowed to embrace her;

Knowing well the blazing consequences…

We had vowed, we had loved,

So we rose;

With sunken eyes and sunken brows

To claim our beloved Sun,

Or fall with blazing wings

Set ablaze by her scorching lips…

N Chinir

You can't expect true love to find you,

When your heart still weeps for skinny love,

Do what you must,

Toss it in the ocean,

Build a bonfire of memories and burn it to ashes,

Burn the whole house down if you have to,

But promise me never to weep for it again…

N Chinir

'A writer's curse'

Isn't it tragically beautiful...
You would let your heart take in all the agony
And in return
You'd bleed out in ink-dipped words;
Hoping that someone out there
Finds comfort in them.

Later on you realize,
No artist could possibly glorify every crack in detail
Nor could rows of sonnet ever map out this labyrinth,
This labyrinth of life;
So you keep filling these pages,
Leaf after leaf;
Conjuring restless seas and shipwreck tides
Until one day you can no more,
Until one day God calls you home,
Until one day you've finally bled out dry.

N. Chinir

One day you won't have to live with chains.

One day you won't have to be afraid of losing your mind,

One day you will let everything out,

Walk in bright light with your horns in full view,

One day you will find your anchor;

One day someone will come up to you and say,

"You know, you can let your demons out to play with mine"

N Chinir

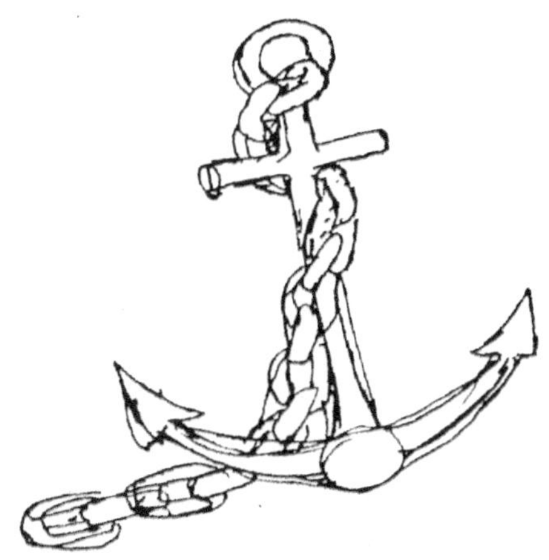

There is a Myth;

Of what happens

After all your heart strings snap;

Some say you would become numb

A few say you would finally become immune to heartaches

She perhaps wanted to put that to test.

N. Chinir

I think most of us are just scared,

And to hide that fear,

We put it under the rug of

"Love is a sham"

"It is a weakness"

Because it went wrong

Once, twice or too many times,

And rightly after the scars in our hearts;

We guarded ourselves well,

Perhaps a little too well sometimes

And later we call it quits,

Proclaiming that the grapes were sour anyways.

N. Chinir

Perhaps Art had always been how our hearts bled out…

Artist, in shades of paints,

Musicians bleeding out in lyrics,

And Poets

Bleeding out in ink.

N. Chinir

She was the dawn

After an endless shade of darkness,

Like warm rays of sunlight

That kisses one's cold skin when snow falls;

Like cigarettes that calms the nerves,

And above all,

That smile of hers,

That could turn any nightmare into sweet dreams…

N. Chinir

I believe we can never truly stop caring for someone,

With whom we have been through everything,

I believe we just become very good at pretending like we don't care…

N. Chinir

It's easy to love the light,

Easy to admire the Sun,

But it takes great courage

To love the darkest corners of your heart,

To forgive yourself for your flaws

And give yourself a pat on the back,

To truly accept what you are

And one day learn to smile,

At all the messed up things that brought you this far.

N. Chinir

'Six of Dice'

We kept it at bay,

With things that will eventually kill us,

Until we found something worth dying for,

Or someone worth dying for,

And we love,

Knowing well that they too are like the drugs that ruin us,

Yet we choose them,

And we start the gamble,

Either a six of dice or a broken heart!

N. Chinir

Some nights you'd hear him speak

About rogue planets,

Planets that don't orbit any star

The rebel planets, the outlaws,

Who have absolute freedom.

To do whatever they want

Who don't follow the laws of physics

Nor any galaxy's,

You'd find him intrigued by the endless possibilities

And the infinite probabilities

After all, there was something darkly alluring

About travelling the entire universe

until the ends of time…

N. Chinir

You know,

The truth is if you look carefully;

Everyone is a little broken.

Pretty faces with sad eyes,

Hundreds of hello

Yet depression kicks in at12

With none to call at 3am

You see,

You may wish to be altruistic enough

And find those broken gems

And polish them until they glow.

But you know,

You can never know for sure

Because people are really good at hiding

Their demons…

That is why it is so important to be kind.

We all sin differently.

N. Chinir

'Stitches'

We belong to a generation filled with scars;

Scars of having to grow up too soon

Scars of committing a little

Too many young mistakes,

We flew too close to the sun

Maybe a little too soon

And now little by little

We all have to relearn how to love ourselves.

N.Chinir

We came by grace, what we become is a choice.

N. Chinir

'Crazy ones'

Fate always fell for the crazy ones,

The ones crazy enough to shoot the sun,

Or swim to the bottom of the lake,

Fly till their wings turned amber,

 In hopes that they could to touch the sun,

She fell in love with mortals

Who were crazy enough to follow their heart and in return

She'd turned them into Stars…

N. Chinir

One day those wounds will be battle scars,
One day you won't have to fill those
Sleepless nights with bloody ink.
One day all your tears will turn to gems,
One day the pain will turn to power…
The sun will rise again,
It's not a hope it's a promise,
Hold on!

N. Chinir

He found peace in the darkness,

She found peace in the light…

She saved him before it consumed him,

He shielded her before she flew too close to the sun.

N. Chinir

'Paper Crowns'

We've come a long way,
From little Kings with paper crowns
To wanting little pieces of the world,

We've come a long way
From venturing out in search of Excalibur
To rescuing damsels in distress,

I believe magic is real,
I also believe that dragons are real,
After all, we did come a long way
From slaying monsters under our bed,

Now only the evil dragon a waits
And they say, it takes the shape of every excuse
We tell ourselves of why we can't be Kings.

N. Chinir

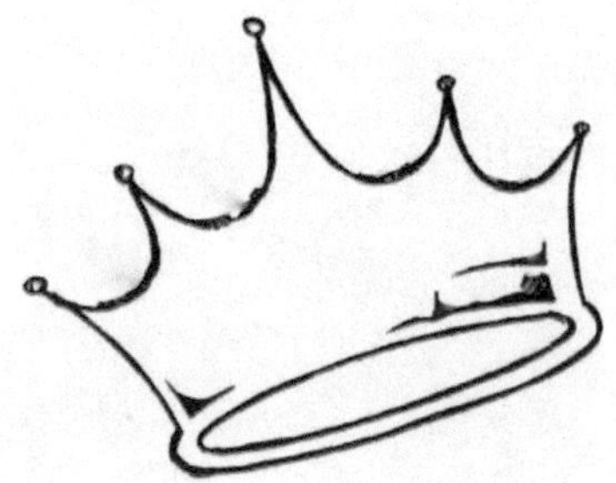

Hopeless Romantic

Wild Flames

Perhaps we are all hopeless romantics;

Enchanted by things,

As dangerous as wildfires,

Perhaps it's the thrill;

That something as precarious

And cataclysmic as wild flames

Can also be marveled for its beauty,

Maybe that's the very reason

Why we humans want love,

The wanting for something

As dangerous as wildfires

So we choose a person

And give them that cataclysmic power,

Power that is capable of destroying us in every way possible,

And we wait…

Either to be burned and destroyed,

Or be loved, like how wild flames love

Laying gentle kisses birthing a beauteous forest.

N. Chinir

Take away those sunlit mornings

But give me those rainy nights

Filled with hot chocolates and old movies

A couple of warm blankets

With my love snuggling under it.

N. Chinir

She was one of the stars

Who got kicked out a constellation,

Cause she would always give away pieces of herself to grant wish-
es...

N. Chinir

One day you'll stumble upon that certain someone,

Who will make you feel everything!

Everything from pain to pleasure

And all in between the lines,

They'll be the reason why you'll be caught smiling,

The very reason

Why you'll start believing in old stories.

N. Chinir

She deserves someone who would make her,

His first and his only one,

With no safety nets,

No second options,

No strings attached…just, her

Just her or a broken heart.

N. Chinir

Maybe Icarus knew exactly what he was doing,

Maybe he felt so in love with the sun,

That all he ever wanted was to touch his love,

Maybe he didn't mind falling with molten feather,

Perhaps he didn't mind drowning for her at all...

N. Chinir

Perhaps we all have a compass in us,

And we take our journey

In hopes to find that place we call home…

And I won't lie

My compass led me to you.

N. Chinir

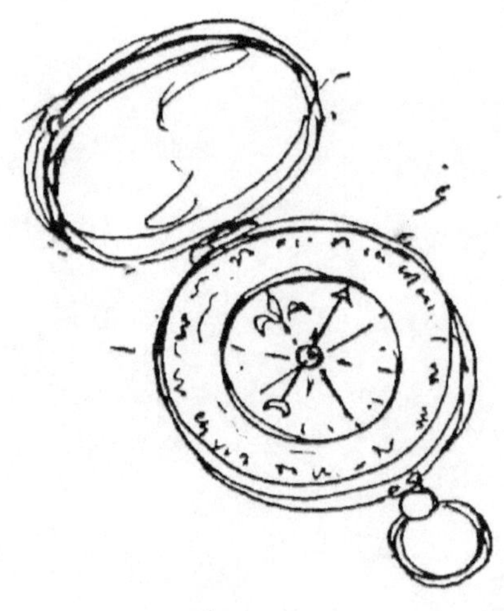

She must have been the descendent of the valkyries…

She picked him up where the world had left him dead,

Perhaps he was the berserk Viking

Fighting for glory!

For Valhalla..!

And she the Valkyrie

Sent by the gods to bring him home…!

N. Chinir

Maybe the storms fell in love with her.
Maybe they have missed her so much that
They' would light up the entire night sky and
Scream out her name over and over again…

N. Chinir

We bleed in poetry;

Gamble in with our hearts

And write whatever the hell our hearts

Secretly confess.

N. Chinir

She was a love that would come,

Offering you both fire and ice,

A sword and a shield,

Sometimes she came like a saint,

Other times she'd drag your soul to the deepest pits of hell,

To love her, you had to be willing to go down in flames…

N. Chinir

She wanted a love that would spread like wild fire,

Beautiful and dangerous.

She wanted a love that would engulf her soul

And kiss every inch of her body, awake.

N. Chinir

He asked her for her heart;

Hands out,

Heart pounding

And eyes longing,

Her lips on his without hesitation

And damn the souls danced…

Danced as if the whole world burned

And all they had was this last kiss…

N. Chinir

"She wanted to truly live…

Live a life where she'd taste the heavens,

And love so wildly and deeply that even if she fell;

She'd fall like a dying star,

Leaving behind trails of magic and stardust

All entangled in a beautiful mess;

She wanted her soul to be scattered all across the universe…"

N. Chinir

'Isabella's Islay'

You were my favorite intoxication,

A sip of you;

Could give a soldier

Dreams of happy endings

You were my Whiskey shots.

Whiskey to console hearts

To hold on for some more sunsets

To keep my nightmares at bay,

In a world full of cheap drinks and wine

You were my bottle of Isabella's Islay.

N. Chinir

Her name was poetry;

Every syllable of her name would fall from your tongue

As if it was your favorite word…

N. Chinir

She tasted of cigarettes and sex,

She claimed as if it was meant to be a description of her…

The golden rule was

 "Never smoke with a person who holds your heart strings",

Cause every time you miss her,

You'd lit up a cigarette,

And try to relive that moment over and over again.

N. Chinir

Sometimes she would get moon drunk,

She'd run around catching fireflies;

Entangling them in her hair

And adorably proclaiming herself

To be one of the stars,

Perhaps she never belonged here,

Perhaps she was one of those fallen celestials,

Who forgot her way home,

Cause she always did look like a fallen piece of heaven…

N. Chinir

You were the dimension
I never knew existed,
Until I accidently brushed your skin,
Until I accidently stumbled upon that smile
Until you came along,
I never knew what haven I longed for,
Until you came along and kissed me awake.

N. Chinir

Dart

You were a proof that even angels could sin…

You'd gaze at the night sky almost longingly;

With your cherry lips on the cigarette tips,

You'd smoke in, as if it was your last midnight cigarette,

Perhaps you were trying your best to forget someone;

Perhaps you did miss heaven

Maybe someone who reminded you of it…

N. Chinir

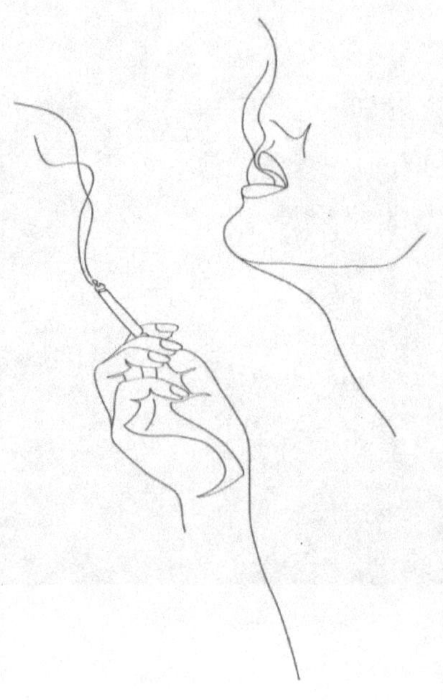

Hell has a thing;

Call it destiny, fate or whatever you may,

But whosoever walks through it,

They change,

Either for the best or worst but in every case

They emerge with hellish flames,

Flames to either destroy or rebuild…

N. Chinir

We all love something that kills us slowly

54

N. Chinir

Heart'

You know why most people lose heart?

Because we took it for granted when it is the rarest thing,

We want it but we don't fight for it,

It only happens when you believe in it,

The saddest truth about this generation,

Is that we over think…

We hope far too much for the wrong ones

And over think far too much for the right ones…

N. Chinir

She'd paint 'Chaos' and 'Apocalypse'

And amidst the storms

She'd search for refuge in the very monsters she breeds…

Maybe she was in love with the storms

Maybe all she ever knew was destruction…

N. Chinir

"Retribution"

There under the melancholy willow
Beside the old church yard, the Ravens crow
Six feet below, there lies three mortal frames
Scorned and stabbed, each heart claiming a stake

The ravens crowed Murderer! Murderer!
Only to heaven shall my soul answer;
Replied the man to the ravens; to their ungodly woe
Why?!... The ungodly voice echoed the grave;
Murderer! Murderer! Cried upon the engraved

The gods know, they earned their cursed stakes,
Blasphemy mortal! Blasphemy! The ungodly woe echoed
The first victim, his gifts, the true sight he forsook;
Hope killed that man not my wretched stake.

The second! The second! His crimes? … They cried,
He forsook pride, he forsook himself, he bowed;
Humility killed that man not my wretched stake,
Pure soul! Pure soul! The ungodly cry followed.

The third! The third! His crime, His crime…?

Desperately, now cried the ravens

He loved, he loved with everything he had;

Love killed that man not my wretched stake,

Now even the dead mourned for this man.

(He stood there while his bodies lay rest,)

The old willows and the grave stood still.

In the deafening silence, a whisper echoed retribution;

Then the Ravens all cried out Retribution! Retribution!

All the voices living and dead monotone in Retribution

We all have that someone,

For whom we'd bend the rules

For whom we'd be willing to do things,

Perhaps for whom we'd fall

Even into the darkest pits of hell;

Only to crawl back up

At the sound of her name…

N. Chinir

She held her agony firm.

Like a paint brush in the hands of an artist,

The elegance, in how her demons danced in her finger tips,

Only a broken heart could see all those monsters

Trapped inside those beautiful brown eyes,

She was by definition, an "Art".

N. Chinir

'The Dance'

Hands outstretched,

And knees bowed,

He looked like a knight asking for a dance…

She would foolishly take his hand

And dance until time went far past eternity,

And the only way she'd pass on was if they stopped dancing…

Perhaps she was a fool;

Perhaps she didn't mind.

That she was dancing with the devil from the very first kiss.

N. Chinir

'Crawl'

Skin to skin and lips to lips

I'll crawl inside you and kiss

Every inch of your skin

Setting it ablaze, tauntingly, gently

And hungrily,

With soft kisses and bites…

I'll love you in ways that you've

Never known mortals could,

And when your mortal frame is pressed

Against mine,

I'll love you so hard

That it will make the demons grin.

N. Chinir

For I'll be here,

Waiting,

For your loaded gun to aim and fire

And for the last time,

You'd listen to my slow instructions

You'd be holding your gun firm;

Calming down your heart,

Taking deep breaths,

And finally…

You'd gently pull the trigger and set me free.

N. Chinir

She wanted power,

She craved it like a dying ember

Craving for a touch of flame,

As if it was her lost love,

And she, the hopeless romantic;

Chasing him to the ends of the earth…

N. Chinir

He craved her like a writer

Desperately craving for a midnight cigarette,

To calm down the midnight demons,

To fucking shut them up;

Before someone else walks out wearing his skin,

She was that cigarette,

That just by pressing it against your lips,

It promised you a mortal haven,

The ecstasy, the bliss, the sin;

And oh how her scent

Could bloody calm the madness and insanity,

She was his cigarette…

And just like that he got addicted to her.

N. Chinir

She was the 3am girl my demons talked about….

The one who brings them to their knees,

The one for whom they won't mind giving up my 3am thoughts to.

N. Chinir

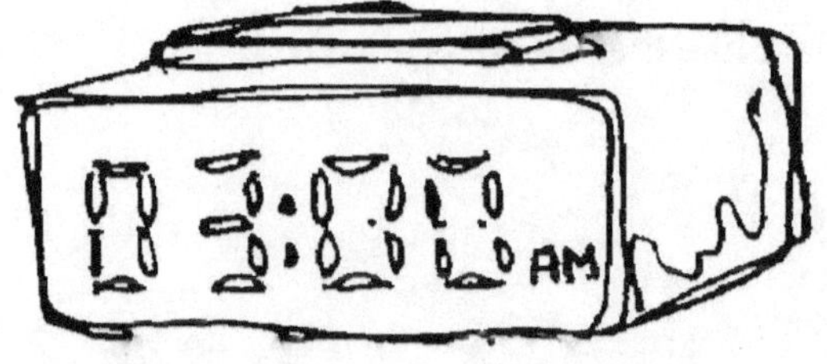

If you haven't noticed,

We just trade one poison for another,

You may give it the sweetest of names

And shower it with hopes,

But at the end, poison does what it does best.

N. Chinir

'Crime'

I wanted to be understood,
And that was my crime.

I wanted to be understood,
Like how you'd understand lowlifes
Like how you'd defend them,
As if you had walked in their footsteps
Reading every thought string
Tracing every decision,
With compassion
With humanity
With love
So I hoped,
Like any wayward soul would.
And damn I wished,
Wished to be flawless
With heroic badges
And perfectly trimmed cuts,

I tried,
My old thoughts, old dreams
Damned and forgotten
Sometimes I wonder if they are lost forever.

But I was still only mundane

Filled with flaws, insecurities and pain.

For God's sake you'd understand the whole world

In all its tainted imperfections,

But your eyes would still be a judge for me.

I wanted to be understood

And that was my crime.

N. Chinir

'Noble-lies'

You'd fight in wars that aren't even yours
You'd brew up storms for people;
Who'd return you with drought
You'd convince yourself it's noble
You'd tell yourself it's alright.
And you'd certainly succeed,
But for how long?
Won't you too die like the others?
Won't those wounds one day bleed you dry
What noble lies will you tell yourself then!

N. Chinir

We all howl to a moon we could never touch

Sometimes that's just how it was written,

You have to learn to accept,

That some things no matter how much you try,

Just aren't meant to be yours.

N. Chinir

'Defeated'

There lay I, bruised and defeated

My sword broken

My will burning low;

Like a dying ember of yore

Father! Father! I looked up to you, waiting

But no Valkyries were sent

Brother why do you avert your gaze,

How does it feel stabbing your own?

To give him to the wolves?

To watch him powerless, scraping for grace,

My throat scorched,

My body no longer my own

I lay waiting for the darkness.

I hear my heart cursing

My thoughts rambling;

Questioning my King, my father, my God!

I must have deserved it

Who will avenge me?

Will they even find my body?

Why should I even live on?

For vengeance! For retribution!

I died that night

But I lived,

Cause broken swords still cut

Bruised knuckles still fight

And scorched wings can still fly.

N. Chinir

Break away

I've torn apart my thoughts,

Rattled the chains you forged

You'd say only vultures rule the sky

And tell me tales of monsters and devils

I worshiped you,

I was naive

But you see,

I have seen the scarlet clouds,

I've seen eagles fly through hurricanes

And establish their rule across the horizons.

So I pray, may those grey clouded memory strings

Be your only witness,

That you once caged a wild thing

A wild soul who rattled the chains

And break away.

N. Chinir

Proud avatars of the night
Reclaim what is yours by right
Oh! Children of the moon
Blessed! Cursed and forsaken,
You whom the gods have hewn
May each strike your hearts awaken,

Fear not Apollo's daylight,
For with hells-fire we rise to fight
The northern bells shall ring
When their souls breathe their last;
When our blades rewrite their past,
And their gods shall bow to us.

N. Chinir

She lit her cigarette,

Counted till three,

And puffed out…

As if she was exhaling

Everything that ever ached her heart

Perhaps she was one of those angels,

Hanging by the mercy of cigarette tips…

N. Chinir

'Petition'

Trust me when I say I've tried it all,
The flairs, the tips
The midnight shots
Even self markings
Yet spells like these don't cure.

Trust me when I say I need a little good
That there are nights when I lose the fight;
Days when someone else takes the wheel
And times when it becomes unclear who's driving
And I sit back and watch it play.

I roll my Sisyphus's bolder
Hoping to alter the loom of fate;
Swimming sometimes drowning but
Never ceasing for a gasp of air,
So trust me when I say I don't need much,
Just enough to keep me going.

N. Chinir

Philosopher

My dream of Peace

Peace, a word filled with assurance,

A word so potent that even souls

Would find tranquility in its brilliance,

Some find peace in calm sunsets;

In the starlit nights of summer's horizon

I find my peace when humanity prospers.

History's chronicles had witnessed

That peace never came without a price.

Generals with their portentous medals preach,

That there is only war and preparation for war.

But have not enough mothers buried their sons?

Have not enough children lost their fathers?

You see them as mere soldiers of war

But I know them as fathers, sons, sisters and brothers

No man was ever conceived with hatred in their heart

We were taught to hate each other

And if we can be taught to hate

We can also be taught to love.

I find my peace when humanity prospers,

I have seen us build pyramids that challenge time

Skyscrapers that touch the sky and cities that never sleeps

We have marked our footprints on the moon,

So, tell me why am I to accept

That peace on Earth is unattainable?

When all of us have never tried together,

Why should only the dead rest in peace?

Why can't the living live in peace?

N. Chinir

Power is neither evil nor good,

It corrupts the weak and makes the ambitious great.

It has just one rule

"You either control it or it controls you".

N. Chinir

The Crown Roads

There lay three roads ahead;

One led to a city of lights and music,

Sirens calling out for attention and acceptance,

Men there walked with plastered smiles

Dissatisfied hollow souls painting a perfect utopia

Men there say "Forget tomorrow and make merry"

Brushing aside the realities of life

They wear their pompous masks perfectly;

All in hopes of achieving the media Crown.

The second path was old and brutish,

Wisdom and perseverance call these woods home,

Men with gleaming eyes and burning wills sought after it;

For only such souls could endure the furnace of creation

Fable souls best shatter just as fable wills do,

For an old promise haunts these woods;

A promise to bestow whoever walked this path

With an everlasting Crown fit for a King.

There lay three roads ahead,

And there lay the last;

 Amidst the ranging storm with gigantic waves,

All the eye could see was Power and Majesty,

There lay God's Grace in simmering gold;

Saints by name and Saints by virtue of deeds

All put their faith on trial,

Until all outstretched hands sank,

And only the pure hearts stood before the true King.

N. Chinir

'Mother'

Wise men say, the hand that rocks the cradle;
Has love that far exceeds the world,
She's the one who bore you till your first cry
The one you owe your first steps to
She's the one, who feels the greatest loss in your last,
The one who picks you up when you fall;
No matter how old you may become

Her heart is a court where every crime is pardoned,
No saint that ever walked the earth could rival her Heart,
Brave soldiers amidst their glorious battle;
Never ceased to bid her goodbye
A soul that personifies the Heavens themselves
And when God calls her noble soul home;
No mortal be selfless enough to let her go,
Yet when her time comes to end,
She would have left behind
Words that turn sons and daughters
Into great men.

N. Chinir

Doctrina vitae

If pride dwells within you,

May pride teach you,

How it burned out the brightest morning star,

But may you be blessed with pride,

When your son becomes a man.

If pain was what you felt,

May your pain teach you

About the pain of others,

So you may learn to see through their smiles

And help those silently wounded.

If hatred was all you knew,

May it teach you about self-destruction

And prove it to you once and for all

That hate has burned the world enough.

If rage was all you ever felt,

Then may it personify hell itself

And your flames be Noble

And your wrath be directed

towards all the injustice and wickedness of the world.

If jealousy was what you felt
May you then, be envious of all the virtues of the righteous,
And in the process
May it teach you to be closer to God.

If love was all you ever knew;
Then know this, the gods are not blind,
They weep for you,
The noblest prayer,
Echoing throughout the universe
Is for a pure heart to never lose hope in humanity;
Even when there are a thousand reasons to do so.
For when the pure hearts lose hope,
God drops the hammer.

And above all may Death, the greatest teacher of all;
Teach you how precious these fleeting seconds are,
So you may learn the significance of life
And cherish it until your heart beats last.

N. Chinir

'Solace'

Some find peace in the silence of *evenings*;

Others amidst the wailing sounds of *War*,

Though our hearts are such indecisive beings,

Peace visited me like warm sunshine

With a pair of chocolate brown eyes,

That held a glimpse of an old armchair;

With an old novel in hand

And little children,

running all around begging for stories.

N.Chinir

When your hands go weary
And your foe stands tall and proud.
When your sword feels heavy
And your armor holds you down,
But the battle rages on.

Your mortal frame barely stands
And the years of training fails you
And your shield pulls you low
But the battle still rages on.

Be valiant enough to strip off your armor,
Pure enough to forsake your pride
And kneel…
Not before men, nor angels
Nor devils nor any saints.

But kneel…
Kneel before He who crowned the shepherd.
Before he who opened the flood gates;
Kneel before the son of man, before God!
And ask, ask humbly for his strength
Ask your father and he shall give you;
The strength bestowed to his children
Who need only ask with a pure Heart.

N. Chinir